CW00456122

It's Easy To Play
Piano Duets.

Wise Publications
London/New York/Sydney

Exclusive Distributors:
Music Sales Limited
8/9 Frith Street, London, W1V 5TZ, England.

Music Sales Pty. Limited
120 Rothschild Avenue, Rosebery, NSW 2018, Australia.

This book © Copyright 1986 by
Wise Publications
ISBN 0.7119.0867.2
Order No. AM 62514

Art Direction by Mike Bell
Cover illustration by Paul Cox
Arranged and compiled
by Frank Booth

Music Sales complete catalogue lists thousands
of titles and is free from your local music
book shop, or direct from Music Sales Limited.
Please send cheque/postal order for £1.50 for postage to
Music Sales Limited, 8/9 Frith Street, London W1V 5TZ.

Unauthorised reproduction of any part
of this publication by any means including photocopying
is an infringment of copyright.

Printed in England by
Caligraving Limited, Thetford, Norfolk

Yesterday

Words and Music by John Lennon and Paul McCartney

Secondo

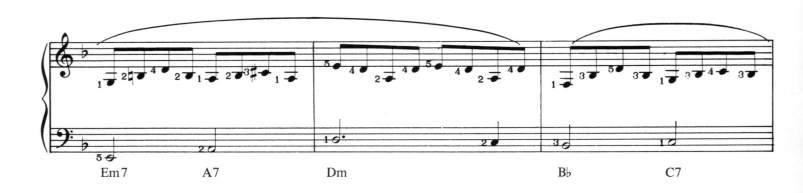

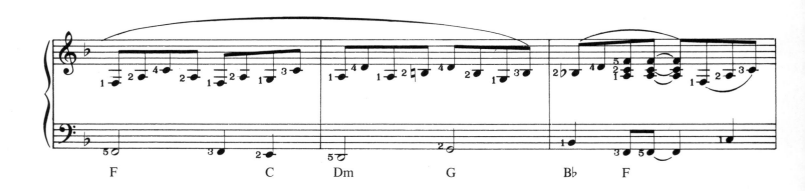

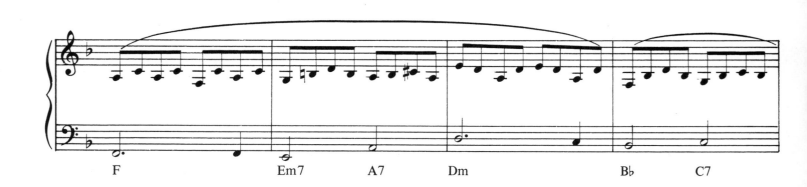

© Copyright 1965 Northern Songs Limited, 3/5 Rathbone Place, London W1.
All Rights Reserved. International Copyright Secured.

Yesterday

Words and Music by John Lennon and Paul McCartney

Primo

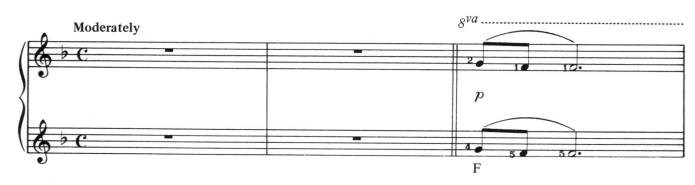

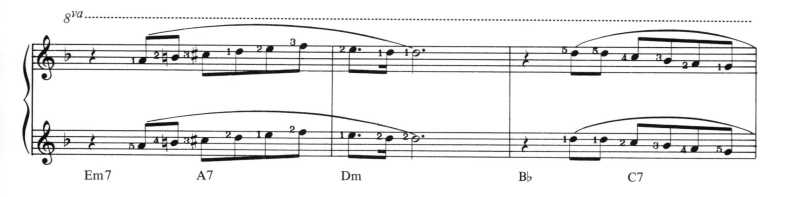

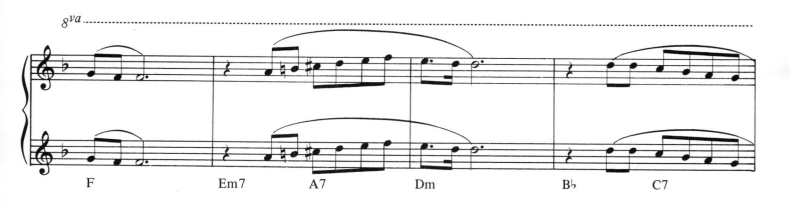

© Copyright 1965 Northern Songs Limited, 3/5 Rathbone Place, London W1.
All Rights Reserved. International Copyright Secured.

Secondo

Primo

Secondo

Primo

Ballade Pour Adeline

Composed by Paul de Senneville

Secondo

© Copyright 1977 Tremplin/Delphine Editions for the world.
Zomba Music Publishers Ltd., 165 Willesden High Road, London NW10 for the UK and Eire.
All Rights Reserved. International Copyright Secured.

Ballade Pour Adeline

Composed by Paul de Senneville

Primo

© Copyright 1977 Tremplin/Delphine Editions for the world.
Zomba Music Publishers Ltd., 165 Willesden High Road, London NW10 for the UK and Eire.
All Rights Reserved. International Copyright Secured.

Secondo

Primo

Michelle

Words and Music by John Lennon and Paul McCartney

Secondo

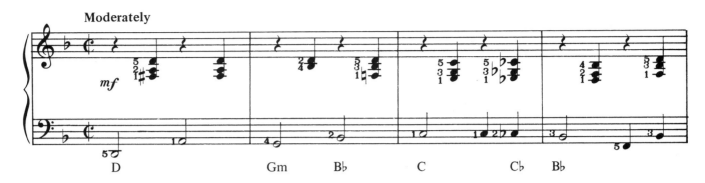

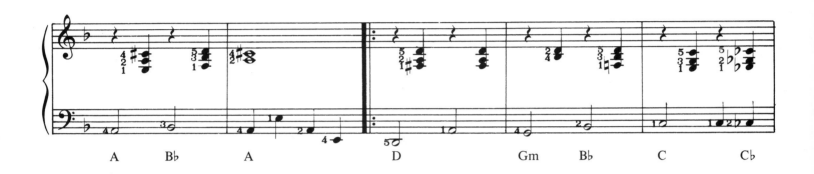

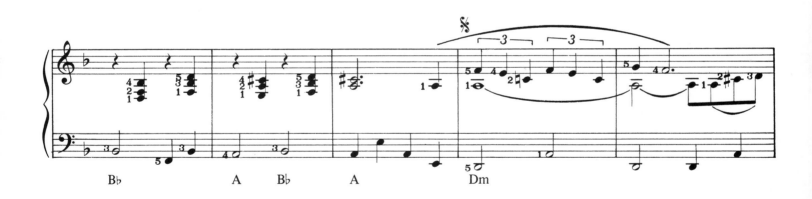

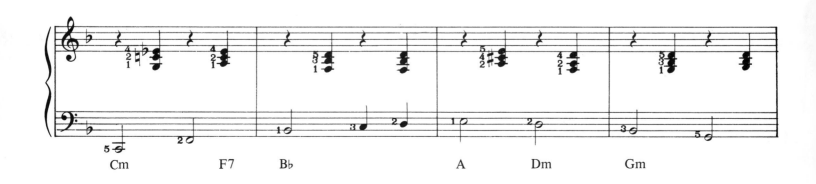

© Copyright 1965 Northern Songs Limited, 3/5 Rathbone Place, London W1.
All Rights Reserved. International Copyright Secured.

Michelle

Words and Music by John Lennon and Paul McCartney

Primo

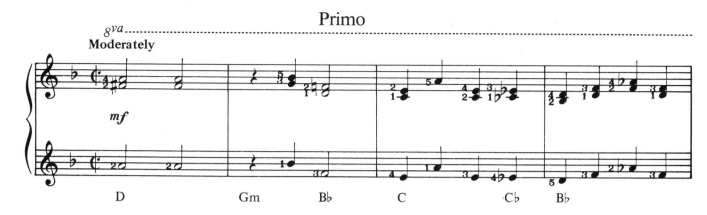

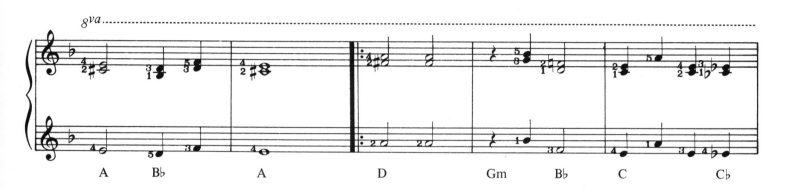

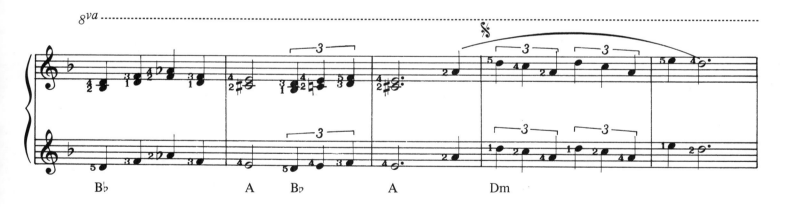

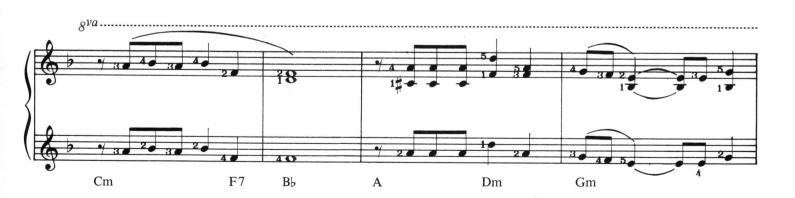

© Copyright 1965 Northern Songs Limited, 3/5 Rathbone Place, London W1.
All Rights Reserved. International Copyright Secured.

Secondo

Primo

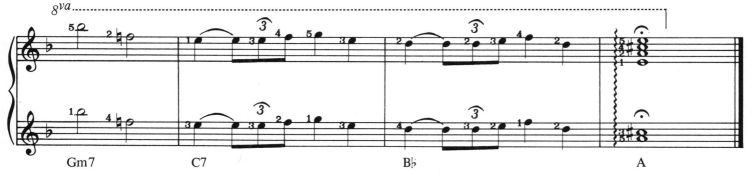

Angela (Theme from "Taxi")

By Bob James

Secondo

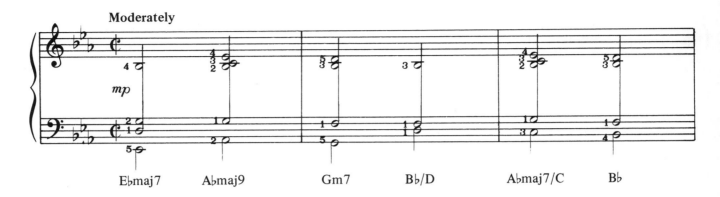

Ebmaj7   Abmaj9   Gm7   Bb/D   Abmaj7/C   Bb

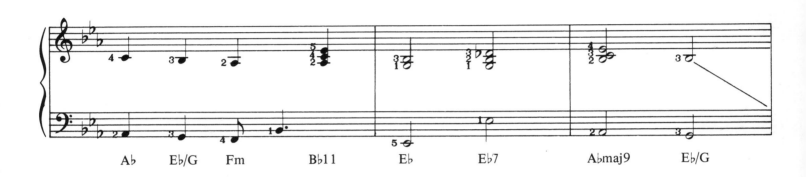

Ab   Eb/G   Fm   Bb11   Eb   Eb7   Abmaj9   Eb/G

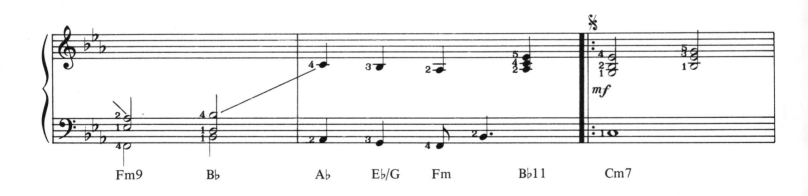

Fm9   Bb   Ab   Eb/G   Fm   Bb11   Cm7

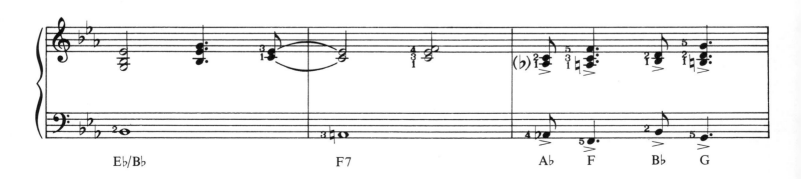

Eb/Bb   F7   Ab   F   Bb   G

© Copyright 1978 Wayward Music Inc. and Addax Music
Co. Inc. (a division of Paramount Pictures Corp.), USA. Used by permission.
All Rights Reserved. International Copyright Secured.

Angela (Theme from "Taxi")

By Bob James

Primo

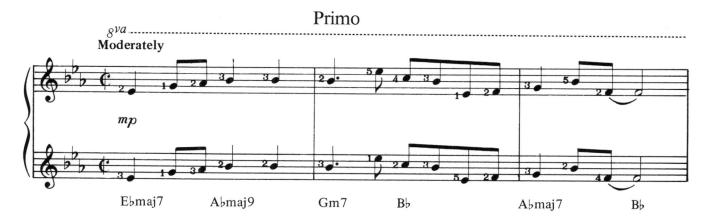

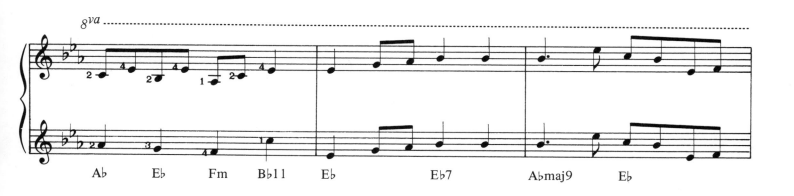

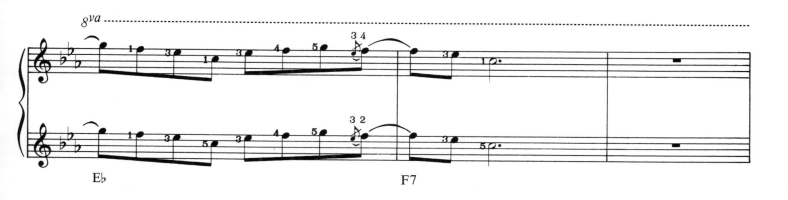

© Copyright 1978 Wayward Music Inc. and Addax Music
Co. Inc. (a division of Paramount Pictures Corp.), USA. Used by permission.
All Rights Reserved. International Copyright Secured.

Secondo

Primo

Secondo

Primo

Sailing

Words and Music by Gavin Sutherland

Secondo

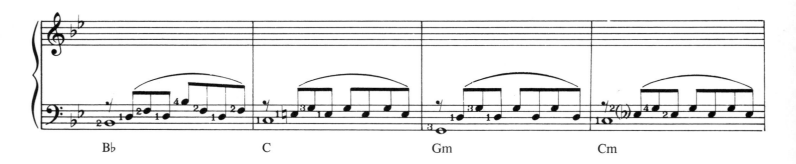

© Copyright 1972 by Island Music Ltd. 334/336 King Street, London W6.
All Rights Reserved. International Copyright Secured.

Sailing

Words and Music by Gavin Sutherland

Primo

© Copyright 1972 by Island Music Ltd. 334/336 King Street, London W6.
All Rights Reserved. International Copyright Secured.

Secondo

Just The Way You Are

Words and Music by Billy Joel

Secondo

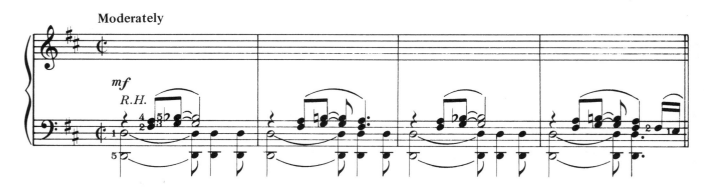

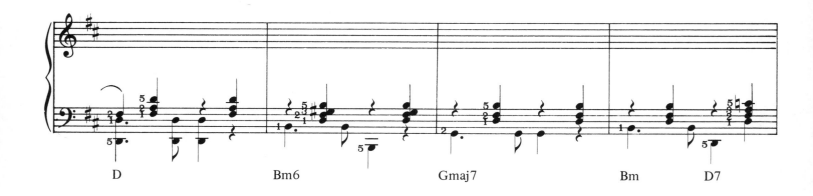

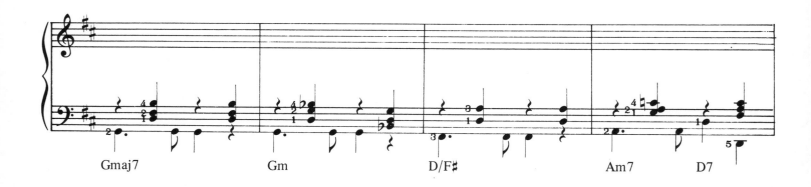

© Copyright 1977 Joelsongs.
Rights assigned to CBS Songs Ltd. for UK, Eire,
Malaysia, Nigeria, Cyprus, India, Pakistan, Ceylon, Ghana, Sierra Leone, Jamaica, Trinidad and Tobago.
All Rights Reserved. International Copyright Secured.

Just The Way You Are

Words and Music by Billy Joel

Primo

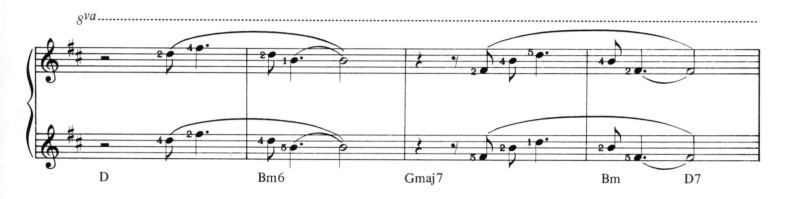

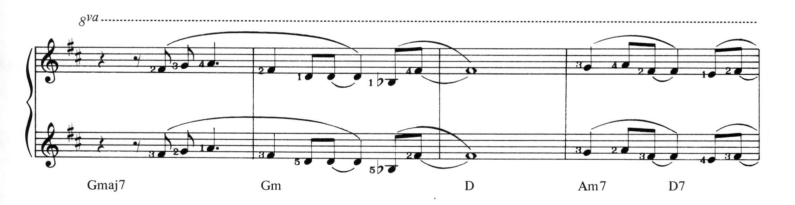

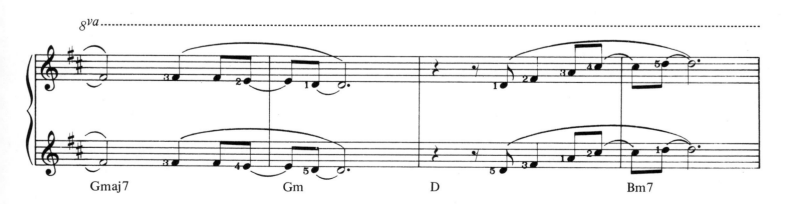

© Copyright 1977 Joelsongs.
Rights assigned to CBS Songs Ltd. for UK, Eire,
Malaysia, Nigeria, Cyprus, India, Pakistan, Ceylon, Ghana, Sierra Leone, Jamaica, Trinidad and Tobago.
All Rights Reserved. International Copyright Secured.

Secondo

Primo

Secondo

32

Primo

Primo

Primo

Bright Eyes

Words and Music by Mike Batt

Secondo

Fairly slowly, with expression

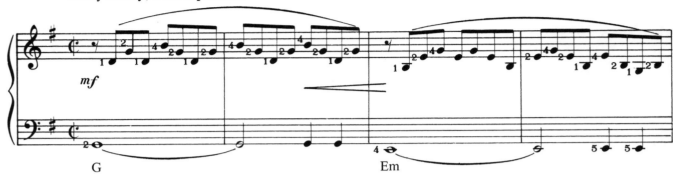

© Copyright 1978 CBS Songs Ltd. Watership Productions, 3/5 Rathbone Place, London W1 for the world.
All Rights Reserved. International Copyright Secured.

Bright Eyes

Words and Music by Mike Batt

Primo

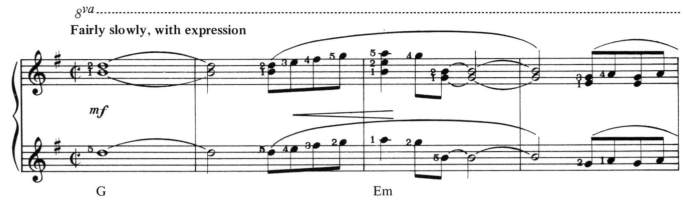

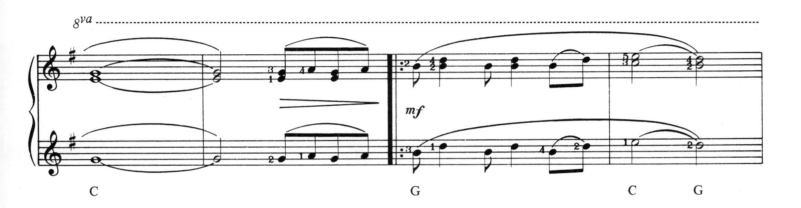

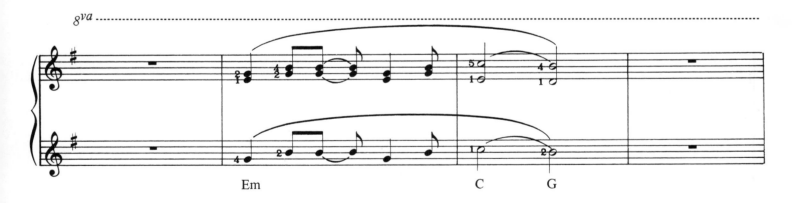

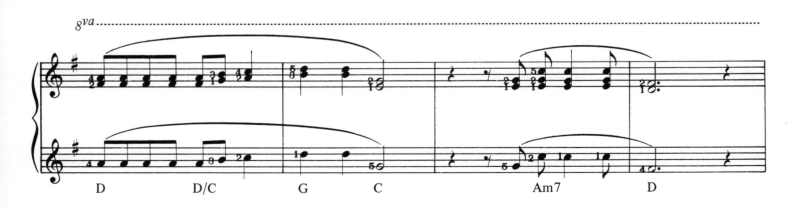

© Copyright 1978 CBS Songs Ltd. Watership Productions, 3/5 Rathbone Place, London W1 for the world.
All Rights Reserved. International Copyright Secured.

Primo

Secondo

42

Annie's Song

Words and Music by John Denver

Secondo

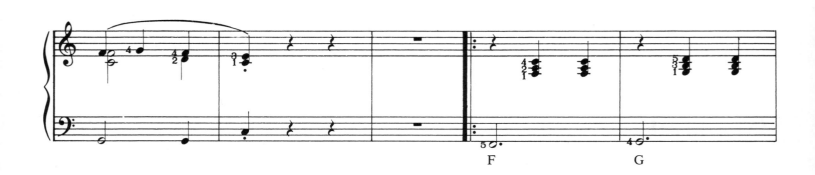

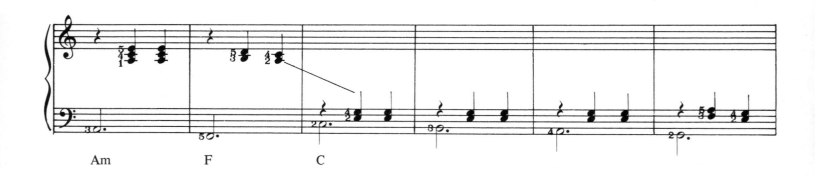

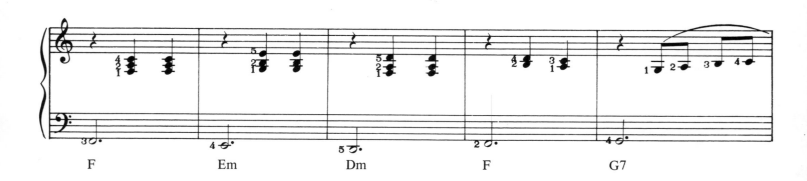

© Copyright 1974 Cherry Lane Music Co. USA.
Cherry Lane Music Ltd., 18/20 Ridgeway, Wimbledon, London SW19
All Rights Reserved. International Copyright Secured.

Primo

The Beatles

Enya

Phil Collins

Van Morrison

Bob Dylan

Sting

Paul Simon

Tracy Chapman

Eric Clapton

Pink Floyd

New Kids On The Block

Bryan Adams

Tina Turner

Elton John

Bee Gees

Whitney Houston

AC/DC

Bringing you the words

All the latest in rock and pop. Plus the brightest and best in West End show scores. Music books for every instrument under the sun. And exciting new teach-yourself ideas like "Let's Play Keyboard" - in cassette/book packs, or on video. Available from all good music shops.

and music

Music Sales' complete catalogue lists thousands of titles and is available free from your local music shop, or direct from Music Sales Limited. Please send a cheque or postal order for £1.50 (for postage) to:

Music Sales Limited
Newmarket Road,
Bury St Edmunds,
Suffolk IP33 3YB

Buddy

Five Guys Named Moe

Les Misérables

West Side Story

Phantom Of The Opera

Show Boat

The Rocky Horror Show

Bringing you the world's best music.